Submarines: Underwater Stealth

Michael Teitelbaum
AR B.L.: 7.0
Points: 1.0   MG

Submarines
Underwater Stealth

Michael Teitelbaum

Enslow Publishers, Inc.
40 Industrial Road
Box 398
Berkeley Heights, NJ 07922
USA
http://www.enslow.com

Library of Congress Cataloging-in-Publication Data

Teitelbaum, Michael.
  Submarines : underwater stealth / by Michael Teitelbaum.
      p. cm. — (Mighty military machines)
  Includes bibliographical references and index.
  ISBN 0-7660-2659-0
  1. Submarines (Ships)—United States—Juvenile literature. I. Title. II.
Series.
  V858.T45 2006
  359.9'30973—dc22

                                    2005034899

Printed in the United States of America

10 9 8 7 6 5 4 3 2 1

To Our Readers:
We have done our best to make sure all Internet Addresses in this book were active and appropriate when we went to press. However, the author and the publisher have no control over and assume no liability for the material available on those Internet sites or on other Web sites they may link to. Any comments or suggestions can be sent by e-mail to comments@enslow.com or to the address on the back cover.

Photo Credits: CORBIS/Steve Kaufman, pp. 19, 22; Department of Defense, pp. 1, 3, 8, 15, 18, 32, 47; Getty Images/Mike Heffner, p. 7; Getty Images/MPI, p. 10; Getty Images/Sandy Huffaker, p. 43; NavSource Naval History/From the collection of W.P. Jones, U.S. Navy photo, p. 26; NavSource Naval History/Photo courtesy of John Hummel, p. 20; U.S. Navy photo, pp. 3, 4, 16, 25, 28, 34, 35, 37, 39, 40 42, 44, 46; XNR Productions, p. 30.

Cover Photos: CORBIS/Steve Kaufman, front; Department of Defense, back.

Contents

Chapter ONE

Attack From Beneath the Sea

In March 2003, four U.S. warships slipped into the Persian Gulf in the Middle East. Hidden hundreds of feet beneath the waters of the gulf, two submarines traveled with the warships. The USS *Cheyenne* was one of those subs.

The ships and submarines were there for a U.S.-led invasion of Iraq. Their mission: To help the United States and its allies remove Iraq's president, Saddam Hussein, from power. On the *Cheyenne*, missile technicians stood ready in the weapons room.

The missile technicians reported that the Tomahawk missile was in position and ready to be fired. Then the fire control technicians took over. These crewmen aimed the weapon, locking it onto its target. All that remained was for the *Cheyenne*'s commanding officer to give the order to fire.

On March 19, 2003, the order was given. The fire control technicians launched the weapon. The Tomahawk missile sped from its vertical launch tube on the *Cheyenne*. Its target was a bunker in Baghdad, Iraq's capital. This bunker was believed to be the hiding place of Saddam Hussein. The missile destroyed the building.

The Tomahawk missile sped from its vertical launch tube on the *Cheyenne*.

Operation Iraqi Freedom had begun. U.S. Marines, soldiers, and bombers took over the assault, invading Baghdad on the ground and bombarding it from the air. Saddam Hussein had not been in the bunker that day. But he was soon found and arrested. His removal from power was a key success in the ongoing war.

The firing of the missile from the USS *Cheyenne* marked the start of the war in Iraq. At the time, a total of four submarines (USS *Cheyenne*, USS *Columbia*, USS *Key West*, and USS *Louisville*) were in the waters off Iraq, firing Tomahawk missiles. Later, a total of eight submarines, each with more than a hundred sailors and twenty missiles, would be stationed in the Middle East. This was the largest number of subs ever deployed to one place by the U.S. Navy.

The USS *Cheyenne*

The USS *Cheyenne* belongs to a class of subs known as the Improved Los Angeles Class. It is the newest submarine in the class, completed in 1996. There are two major types of U.S. submarines, and many different classes within each type.

The *Cheyenne* and other Improved Los Angeles Class subs are fast-attack subs, known as SSN type. The "SS" means that the vessel is a submarine. The

FACT FILE

How Nuclear Power Works

All nuclear-powered submarines have a nuclear reactor, which generates the electricity that runs the sub. In the reactor, nuclear power is created when the atoms of a metal called Uranium-235 split apart. The splitting of the atoms creates heat. This heat is used to boil water, which creates steam. The steam provides power to turn a turbine, which then turns an electrical generator. The generator makes enough electricity to operate the sub. Uranium-235 is a very dangerous material, but if the nuclear reactor is properly maintained and operated it can be used as a safe source of power.

▲ Sailors secure the USS *Boise* to the pier in Norfolk, Virginia, in April 2003. The sub had just returned from its mission launching Tomahawk missiles during Operation Iraqi Freedom.

"N" means that it is nuclear powered. The main use of fast-attack subs is pursuing opposing subs and ships and attacking them with missiles.

The other major type of submarine is the fleet ballistic nuclear missile submarine, known as an SSBN type. The "B" means that these subs carry ballistic missiles, which carry nuclear weapons capable of destroying entire cities.

FACTFILE

Improved Los Angeles Class Submarines

Completed: 1995–1996
Size: *Length:* 360 feet; *Width:* 33 feet
Power source: one pressurized water (steam generating)
   nuclear reactor
Maximum operating depth: 1,480 feet
Maximum time underwater: 90 days
Maximum speed: 20 knots (23 miles per hour)
Number of torpedoes/missiles: 22 (including
   12 Tomahawk missiles)

In addition to performing missions like the one in Iraq, the Improved Los Angeles Class subs can also be used for several other purposes. They can attack other subs in direct combat. They can also deliver special forces troops, such as U.S. Navy SEALs. Today's Improved Los Angeles Class subs gather intelligence,

◀ The USS *Pogy* and its crew went to the Arctic Circle in 2000 to do scientific research. The large "sail" on the top of the sub helped the *Pogy* break through six inches of Arctic ice.

which is information about the opposing side's plans or weapons. They also perform search-and-rescue missions for pilots who have crashed at sea. Improved Los Angeles Class subs are also Arctic capable. This means that, unlike earlier subs, they can travel under the ice in the Arctic region. A hard, ice-breaking "sail" attached to the sub can cut through the layer of ice on top of the ocean. Then, the subs can go to the surface and travel in these frozen parts of the world.

FACTFILE

What Is Sonar?

The sonar equipment on a submarine acts as the vessel's eyes and ears when the sub is deep in the dark ocean. It is used to detect the presence and location of objects (usually other subs or ships) under the sea. "Sonar" stands for <u>So</u>und <u>Na</u>vigation and <u>R</u>anging.

There are two types of sonar, active and passive. With active sonar, a sub sends a sound pulse out into the water and crewmen listen to see how long it takes for the pulse to bounce off another object and return to the sub. This tells the crew how far away and in what direction the other sub or ship is. If a sub uses active sonar, the sonar on any other sub or ship in the area will detect it and know the sub is out there.

Since the main goal of a sub is to stay hidden and operate in secret, most subs rarely use active sonar. Instead, they use passive sonar. This consists of listening for sounds made by other ships and subs. A skilled sonar operator can figure out another ship's speed and even what kind of ship it is, just by listening to the passive sonar.

Chapter TWO

What Are Submarines?

Today, when we think of submarines, we picture huge metal vessels. We know that they are filled with hi-tech equipment. But the earliest submarines date back to the 1600s. Early designs in Ukraine and Holland were little more than large, hollow, wooden balls. They had breathing tubes that went to the water's surface.

The first military submarine was the *Turtle*, built in 1775. It was also the first American sub. The *Turtle* was about seven and a half feet long, six feet tall, and three feet wide. Shaped like a giant clam, it was made from two wooden shells covered with tar.

It submerged by allowing water into its hull, or body. Two hand-cranked propellers moved the sub up and down and side-to-side. To surface, the operator had to pump the water out by hand. This made the *Turtle* lighter so it would rise.

In 1776, during the American Revolution, David Bushnell, the *Turtle*'s inventor, attempted to use it to sink a British warship in New York harbor. While underwater, he tried to attach a gunpowder-filled torpedo to the underside of the ship. But the torpedo did not attach properly and did no damage to the British vessel.

During the American Civil War, in the 1860s, the Union Army used a twenty-man sub called the *Alligator*. The forty-seven-foot-long sub was originally powered by oars, but later was given hand-operated propellers. The operator in the sub turned a crank, which then turned the outside propellers to power the ship.

Shaped like a giant clam, the *Turtle* was made from two wooden shells covered with tar.

The *Alligator* was the first sub to include an airlock from which a diver could exit a sub while underwater to attach mines, or small explosive devices, to enemy ships. An airlock is a small room which can be filled with air or water. When a diver is going to leave a sub, the room is filled with water.

Then the door is opened and the diver goes out into the sea. When the diver returns, he enters the airlock, which is again filled with water. The outer hatch is then closed and the water is pumped out of the airlock. Then the crew opens the inside door and the diver steps back into the sub. Without an airlock the sub would flood each time a diver went in or out.

From Gasoline to Nuclear Power

A "modern" submarine was invented in the late 1890s. In 1900, the U.S. Navy bought the sub, calling it the USS *Holland* after its inventor, John Phillip Holland. The *Holland* was the first submarine to use a gasoline-powered engine while on the surface, and electric battery power for traveling underwater.

In 1904, the French submarine *Aigrette* replaced the gasoline-powered engine with a diesel-powered engine for surface travel. This remained the standard submarine power system for the next fifty years. In 1949, Navy Admiral Hyman G. Rickover oversaw the development of nuclear power for submarines. Rickover was called the "Father of the Nuclear Navy." His work led to the creation of the world's first nuclear powered submarine, the USS *Nautilus*, in 1955.

Before the use of nuclear power on submarines, subs were forced to surface regularly. They needed to fill up with diesel fuel and recharge their electric batteries. Subs also needed to surface frequently to re-supply themselves with oxygen so the crewmen could breathe.

Around the same time that nuclear power was added to subs, oxygen generators, which can take oxygen right from seawater, were also created. These two changes allowed submarines to remain underwater for months at a time. They no longer needed to surface to refuel and get fresh air.

Most improvements in submarine design since the 1950s have had to do with the type and number of weapons they are capable of carrying. Since the

FACTFILE

Water and Air

Imagine being underwater on a submarine for two months. You would need oxygen to breathe and fresh water to drink. Both of these can be taken from the ocean water that surrounds the submarine.

Salt water from the ocean is heated until it becomes vapor, which eliminates the salt. The vapor is then cooled and collected as fresh drinking water. Oxygen generators remove oxygen from seawater, releasing breathable air.

Keeping the air on a sub clean is also important. When people breathe, they exhale a gas called carbon dioxide. Breathing in too much carbon dioxide can be deadly. Because of this, the air on board a sub must be "scrubbed." It passes through filters called "scrubbers," which remove the carbon dioxide, leaving only clean oxygen to breathe.

1990s, new submarine designs have also reflected changing computer technology.

How Subs Work

All submarines contain large tanks called ballast tanks. When the ballast tanks are filled with air, the submarine floats on the ocean's surface, like a regular ship. In order to submerge, a submarine fills its ballast tanks with water. The extra weight from the water causes the sub to sink. When it is time to come back up, the sub blows thousands of gallons of water out of its tanks and rises to the surface.

Submarines are steered from the control room. The helmsman adjusts the rudder, flaps that steer the sub left or right. The planesman adjusts the diving planes, flaps that steer the sub up or down.

When a sub is near the surface it can raise its periscope, which allows crewmen to see if there are ships or land nearby. When a sub is underwater sonar helps the sub's crew make their way through the darkness beneath the sea.

The Crew

A modern submarine like the *Cheyenne* carries a crew of 134 people. The crew is made up of 13 officers, who are in command, and 121 enlisted men, who perform the day-to-day work that keeps the sub running.

The crew is divided into different groups based on their jobs. The executive department is in charge of making sure everyone else does their job so that missions go smoothly. The sub's commanding officer, or captain, is in charge of everything that happens on the sub. Every department reports to the captain.

The engineering department makes sure that the sub's nuclear reactor operates safely. Taking care of the ship's torpedoes, missiles, and sonar equipment is the job of the weapons department. The torpedoman's mate, missile technician, and fire control technician all work in the weapons department.

On board the USS *Annapolis*, the planesman (third from left) ▼ works the diving planes that move the sub up and down in the water. Other technicians work close by.

▲ A Navy officer peers into the periscope on the USS *Norfolk* to see what is on the surface of the water around the sub.

The sub's position is monitored at all times by the operations department. They are also responsible for the communications equipment.

The ship's food and spare parts are managed by the supply department. They cook all the meals for the crew, and also take care of the crew's laundry.

Taking care of the crew's health is the job of the medical department. They give the crew regular check-ups and treat them when they are sick. They also inspect the sub every day to make sure it is clean, and check the quality of drinking water, food, and air so the crew stays healthy.

Weapons

Modern subs have four different types of weapons: MK-48 torpedoes, Harpoon missiles, Tomahawk (cruise) missiles, and submarine-launched mobile mines (SLMMs). An MK-48 torpedo operates underwater. It can be used against ships or other submarines.

A Harpoon missile is designed to skim the ocean's surface, then strike and sink warships. Once it is fired, a Harpoon missile's radar automatically turns on to help the missile find its target. The Tomahawk (cruise) missile flies through the air toward a target on land, such as a building.

A submarine-launched mobile mine (SLMM) is used like a torpedo, but only in shallow water. It is used to target opposing submarines.

Living Underwater

Today, the amount of time a submarine can stay underwater is only limited by the food supply and how long the crew can do their jobs well without a break back on land. That is usually about two months.

On a submarine, a day is eighteen hours long, not twenty-four hours long. Since the sub's crew does not see daylight or nighttime they very quickly get used to this schedule. The eighteen-hour day is divided into three six-hour work shifts called watches. Each crewman is on duty for six hours doing his job. Then he is off duty for twelve hours.

During his off time a crewman will sleep, eat, shower, exercise, attend training sessions, study for promotions, watch movies, or play cards. Subs keep about four hundred movies on board. They also carry board games, video games, and books.

Crewmen also spend a lot of their off-duty time cleaning the sub. Imagine more than one hundred people living together in a small space for two months. Things can get pretty dirty if they are not taken care of. The floors, or decks, are scrubbed, and equipment and living areas are cleaned each day.

Crewmen eat breakfast, lunch, and dinner every day. Crewmembers going on or coming off watch also eat midnight rations (nicknamed "midrats"). Eggs, pancakes, and cereal are served for breakfast. Deli sandwiches, hamburgers, and pizza are made for lunch. Pasta, steak, chicken, and pork dishes are cooked for dinner. Leftovers are eaten for midrats. Treats like ice cream and soda are also always available.

Crewmen sleep in a section of the sub called the berthing area. Each crewman gets about fifteen

▼ When sailors are off duty and their sub has surfaced, there might even be time for a swim! These sailors are leaping off the USS *Portsmouth* into the Pacific Ocean.

square feet of space in which to sleep and store his personal belongings. Each crewman's bed (also called a bunk, berth, or rack) has a small reading light. Personal belongings are stored in a locker under the bunk. Some bunks are so small that there is not enough room for a crewman to turn over without getting out of bed and getting back in!

A submarine operates around the clock, so about one third of the crew is always sleeping while the others work. Because of this, lights in the berthing area are kept dim. The commanding officer has a cabin. All other officers have staterooms, in which they work and sleep.

On land, submarine crewmen wear the regular white uniforms worn by all sailors in the Navy. While on the sub, they wear one-piece blue coveralls.

Working and living together, the crew of a submarine form a special group well trained for the operation of the complex machinery of a modern submarine, and for life under the sea.

Sailors get used to ▼ the close quarters on a sub, including the berthing area.

Chapter THREE

Run Silent, Run Deep: The USS *Permit*

The development of technology such as nuclear power and oxygen generators allowed submarines to take on longer missions. They could stay underwater for long periods of time, silent and unseen. This was extremely important during what was known as the Cold War Era (1945–1989).

During this time it was important for the United States to keep an eye on the ships and subs of its rival, the former Soviet Union. Both countries had nuclear weapons aimed at each other. These destructive weapons could have wiped out either country if fired. Because of this, tension between the powerful nations was high. Many people lived in fear.

The Cold War was not a conflict in which enemies attacked each other. It was a time of spying, gathering information, and keeping a watchful eye on the opposing side. This was a job for submarines.

Such a job was taken on by the USS *Permit* in 1980. Early that year, the *Permit* set off on a six-month assignment patrolling the Pacific Ocean. It traveled from San Diego in Southern California up to Washington State in the Pacific Northwest. The *Permit* belonged to a class of fast-attack subs also called *Permit*.

Tension between the powerful nations was high. Many people lived in fear.

The cigar-shaped sub bounced furiously as it pulled away from the San Diego naval base. Rough seas tossed the sub as it cruised along the ocean's surface.

When the *Permit* was safely away from the dock, the order to submerge was given. Water filled the ballast tanks, replacing the air that had kept the ship afloat. The submarine began to dive and was soon deep under the ocean.

The *Permit*'s mission was to silently, secretly keep an eye out for Soviet submarines in the Pacific Ocean using passive sonar and remaining hidden. The Soviets sent their subs in to try and learn the location and number of U.S. warships stationed on the west coast. The job of the *Permit* was to make sure that the Soviets did not get this important information.

In this mission, a good deal of time was spent searching, listening, waiting, and doing nothing. It could be boring, even though the crew knew that their mission was a valuable one. Crew members played cards and board games. They watched movies to break up the boredom of day-to-day life on the sub. Meanwhile, the various crewmen

▼ Cooks on board the USS *Olympia* work together in the sub's tiny kitchen, preparing a meal for their fellow sailors.

performed their usual duties, keeping the sub operating smoothly.

The technicians who took care of the nuclear reactor on the *Permit* were nicknamed the "Nukes." The Nukes were responsible for checking the reactor's radiation levels to make sure that the crew was safe from the dangerous nuclear radiation generated by the reactor. They also made sure the steam created by the reactor was at the correct pressure.

The radioman worked to keep the *Permit* in communication with other subs, as well as its base back in San Diego.

The crewmen nicknamed the "A-Gang" operated the auxiliary machinery, including systems that supplied fresh drinking water and fresh air to the crew. The cooks in the "mess," or dining hall, planned and cooked the meals for the entire crew. The storekeepers were in charge of supplies, from food to spare parts to other equipment.

When a report would come in that a Soviet sub might be in the area, the *Permit*'s sonarman, in charge of monitoring the sub's sonar, went to work. The main part of the sonarman's job was to listen.

Every submarine makes a different sound, called a noise signature. This is created by the sub's onboard machinery, hull vibrations, and the turning of its propellers. These movements send sound waves out into the water which are picked up by the sonar of other subs. The job of the *Permit* was to use its sonar to identify any noise signatures they came across. The sonarman on board was specially trained to recognize noise signatures. Using both sounds and sound wave patterns which appear on sonar screens, he determined what type of sub they came from.

Whenever a Soviet sub was detected the crew of the *Permit* made their presence known by sending out an active sonar signal. Once the Soviets realized that they had been discovered in U.S. waters, they would turn and flee. Neither sub would be looking for a fight. If the *Permit* could chase a Soviet sub away from the Pacific coast of the United States before it had a chance to learn anything about U.S. warships, then its mission was a success.

FACTFILE

The USS *Permit*

Completed: 1967
Size: *Length:* 278 feet, 6 inches; *Width:* 31 feet, 8 inches; *Height:* 25 feet, 2 inches
Power source: one pressurized water (steam generating) nuclear reactor
Maximum operating depth: 1,300 feet
Maximum time underwater: 90 days
Maximum speed: 25 knots (29 miles per hour)
Number of torpedoes/missiles: 4

Like these sailors, the *Permit's* sailors played card games ▲ during their 1980 mission. This helped fill the long hours between Soviet submarine sightings.

Living and working together so closely underwater for more than a month at a time often led to tension among the crew. However, it also bred loyalty and a sense of teamwork. Each member of the crew knew that he needed the others to make the sub run safely. Working together, playing games, watching movies, and spending off-duty time together led to a true sense of comradery.

The *Permit* served until 1991, when it was decommissioned, or taken out of service.

Chapter FOUR

Listening In:
The USS *Halibut*

Navy Captain James Bradley sat alone in his office in Washington, D.C. It was 3:00 A.M. The rest of the building was quiet. But the plan forming in Captain Bradley's mind had him excited and unable to sleep.

The year was 1970. The Cold War was about to enter its third decade. Captain Bradley believed that if his plan was successful, it would change the course of history and give the United States the upper hand in the Cold War.

Captain Bradley planned to send the submarine USS *Halibut* on a secret mission. The *Halibut* had been built in 1960 as the only sub in its very own class. It was the first sub designed to carry guided missiles, which use built-in radar to find their targets.

The *Halibut* would be sent to the Sea of Okhotsk off the eastern coast the Soviet Union. There, in the heart of Soviet-controlled territory, its crew would search the seafloor for a target no more than five inches wide. They were looking for a telephone cable that ran from a Soviet missile submarine base all the way to Moscow, the Soviet capital, about 3,700 miles away. (That is about the same distance from New York City to Paris, France!) Captain Bradley knew that if they could tap into the cable, the United States would be able to listen to top-secret Soviet military information.

Secrecy and silence would be the keys to the success of this plan.

Secrecy and silence would be the keys to the success of this plan. And nothing was more suited for this type of work than a submarine. In fact, this mission was so secretive that of the 111 men on board, only the sub's commander, Jack McNish, his 14 officers, and the handful of deep-sea divers on the special projects team knew the purpose of the *Halibut's* operation. The others were told that the divers were there to search for pieces of Soviet missiles.

FACTFILE

Decompression

The water pressure under the sea is much greater than the air pressure on land because of the weight of the water above. When deep-sea divers leave a submarine to explore the ocean's bottom, their bodies must already be used to the increased pressure. A decompression chamber is used to slowly increase the pressure for divers before they leave the sub.

Then, the process is reversed when the divers return. The pressure is slowly lowered in the chamber and the divers are given oxygen to breathe before they step back into the normal air pressure aboard the sub. If pressure changes too quickly, divers can experience what is known as "the bends." The body releases gas bubbles into the bloodstream that cause difficulty in breathing, and can even lead to death.

FACTFILE

The USS *Halibut*

Completed: 1960
Size: *Length:* 360 feet; *Width:* 29 feet, 6 inches;
      Height: 20 feet, 9 inches
Power source: one Westinghouse S3W nuclear reactor
Maximum operating depth: about 700 feet
Maximum time underwater: 90 days
Maximum speed: 15.5 knots (17.9 miles per hour)
Number of torpedoes/missiles: 11

The divers on board the *Halibut* would leave the sub when it was on the seafloor. There, they would battle the incredible pressure and strong currents near the sea's bottom and attempt to place a recording device onto the Soviet communications cable.

The sub carried special equipment just for this difficult operation. Because the mission was top-secret, this equipment was also kept secret. One such item was the deep-sea divers' decompression chamber. This would allow the divers to prepare for and recover from their underwater mission.

The other piece of special equipment was nicknamed the "fish." This was a device containing a video camera, a photo camera, and lights, which were all attached to a cable. The fish was sent out of the sub so it could search the sea bottom for the Soviet communications cable. Once it found the cable, it would send videos and photos back to the sub.

Arriving in the Sea of Okhotsk, the *Halibut* stayed close enough to the surface to use its periscope. As the sub glided along the Soviet shoreline, Commander McNish peered through the periscope, searching for something on the shore. He knew that the Soviets' underwater cable would be marked with a sign so that ships passing near the shore would not accidentally tear the cable.

▼ During the Cold War, there was a Soviet communications cable on the floor of the Sea of Okhotsk. It carried messages from a submarine base to Moscow, the Soviet capital, thousands of miles away.

McNish found the sign and gave the order for the *Halibut* to submerge. He then ordered the special projects team to launch the fish. The small cluster of cameras and lights motored slowly through the dark water, attached to its long cable. For several days, the fish sent back grainy photos and video images of giant crabs and tiny jellyfish.

Only the handful of men who were part of the special projects team were allowed to view these images. The men watched closely, searching for any signs of the Soviet communications cable. About a week after they started searching, the fish sent back images of a bump in the sea's

The *Halibut* had found the cable at last!

floor. Along the bump, like the black dashes of a dotted line, the cable stuck out of the sandy bottom. The *Halibut* had found the cable at last!

The *Halibut*'s crew now had to find a flat stretch of sea bottom near the cable. They stopped the sub above a long flat area, then slowly lowered its two large mushroom-shaped anchors to the seafloor. These would keep the *Halibut* from drifting.

The divers had been waiting in the secret decompression chamber for many hours. Their bodies had to slowly get used to the increased water pressure they would face on the sea's floor.

When they were ready, the divers slipped into rubber suits. Tubes ran through the suits. One tube

▲ A Navy diver inspects part of a wrecked ship off the coast of the United States. Like the divers from the *Halibut*, this one wears a specially equipped suit to help him survive and work on the ocean floor.

brought oxygen to the divers' helmets. Another carried communications lines so they could stay in contact with Commander McNish on the sub. One set of tubes contained hot water, which kept the divers warm in the cold seawater.

The suits also contained an emergency line, which could be used to pull the divers back into the sub if something went wrong with their mission. The divers also carried small bottles of emergency air, nicknamed "come-home bottles." These would allow them to breathe for about four minutes if their main oxygen supply failed, enough time to make it back to the sub in an emergency.

Commander McNish gave the order, and the divers slipped from the decompression chamber and out into the sea. They worked for many hours, attaching a recording device to the cable.

Back in the *Halibut*, the helmsman and planesman took readings of the water currents every fifteen minutes. They struggled to keep the *Halibut* steady as the sub swayed against its anchors, pulled by the powerful deep-sea currents.

Finally the divers had successfully completed their task. Top-secret Soviet phone calls were now being recorded by the United States. The divers returned safely to the *Halibut*. They spent a few hours in the decompression chamber to get their bodies back to normal. Then the USS *Halibut* headed for home, its mission successfully completed.

The *Halibut* was decommissioned in 1976 and mothballed, or put in storage. Then, in 1994, this important "weapon" in the Cold War was scrapped. The *Halibut* was taken apart and its metal was recycled. This is common with older military equipment and does not lessen the valuable service it performed while it was in active use.

Chapter FIVE

Submarines Today and in the Future

The role of submarines has changed throughout history as technology has allowed these amazing vehicles to do more and more. The U.S. Navy lists three major reasons why submarines are important to the defense of the United States.

The first reason is stealth. This is the ability to move quietly and secretly. The second is agility. This is the ability to travel quickly and easily to places no other vehicle can reach. The third is endurance. This is the ability to remain on patrol, hidden, for long

◀ Unmanned Undersea Vehicles (UUVs) like this one, the *Blue Fin*, use the latest technology to explore dangerous waters. Using UUVs, missions can be carried out without putting sailors at risk.

periods of time. Submarines can slip into the most highly guarded regions of the world, undetected. They can carry missiles capable of destroying another submarine, a ship, or a target on land.

As submarines are used more often in dangerous war zones, the threat to their crews grows greater. Underwater mines are a constant danger. So are anti-ship cruise missiles fired from other subs.

FACT FILE

Navy SEALs

The Navy SEALs have been operating since 1962. SEAL stands for SEa, Air, and Land. These special forces are usually the first ones to go into dangerous situations. They clear the way for other troops. The SEALs undergo what many consider to be the toughest military training in the world.

In addition to mission training and practice working as a team, each SEAL must endure grueling fitness training. A typical SEAL workout includes swimming five hundred yards in eight minutes, doing a hundred push-ups in two minutes, and running a mile and a half in under ten minutes. Like the submarines that sometimes carry them to their dangerous destinations, SEALs are powerful, impressive, and operate in stealth and secrecy.

Computer and communications systems work together to make submarines safer and better at what they do. Through Internet-like hook-ups using satellites, submarines can instantly share voice and data information with other subs, ships, and planes. In the future, these systems will operate even faster.

Technicians are working to connect certain systems on board subs so the systems will operate together and make all kinds of information readily available to the crewmen who use them. These systems include sonar, which helps locate targets underwater, and radar, which sends out radio waves to help locate targets in the air and on the ground. Voice communications systems, weapons systems, and computer data information systems will also be part of this network. New sonar equipment will be better at detecting mines and icebergs under the sea in time to safely move away from these dangers.

UUVs are like robots and do not need a crewman to operate them from the inside.

Unmanned Undersea Vehicles (UUVs) will allow sub crews to explore the most dangerous waters without putting any crewmen in danger. The vehicles are like robots and do not need a crewman to operate them from the inside. They are launched from the sub in areas with very shallow water. They can also be used in places known to have

Virginia Class Subs

The newest and best fast-attack submarines ever built for the U.S. Navy are the Virginia Class subs. They are the first subs designed for a variety of open-ocean and close-to-shore missions.

One thing that helps with these missions is a new type of periscope. Instead of a traditional periscope, Virginia Class subs use two photonics masts, which extend up from the hull. Each of these masts contains several high-resolution digital cameras equipped with infrared sensors. Infrared technology allows pictures to be taken even in very low light.

Signals from the photonics masts are sent through fiber optic cables (like the ones used for phone and Internet connections on land) to computers on board the subs. The signals provide images that can be shared via a computer network with other subs, ships, or people on land.

Developed during the late 1990s and early 2000s, the first Virginia Class sub, the USS *Virginia*, was put into service in June 2004 and is in use today. Below, a sailor operates the *Virginia*'s engine.

many mines. UUVs will allow future submarines to take on more dangerous missions without as much danger to human lives.

The use of modular technology will allow crews on future subs to update their equipment quickly.

FACTFILE

What Happens to an Old Submarine?

When the Navy feels that an old submarine is no longer worthy of being in the fleet, that sub is decommissioned, or retired. Some decommissioned subs are scrapped and their metal recycled. This was the case for both the USS *Permit* and the USS *Halibut*. The dangerous nuclear reactors on subs used to be disposed of at sea. Now they are buried in special nuclear waste dumps in Oregon and Washington State.

Other subs are given to the U.S. Maritime Administration. These subs are used in case of a national emergency. They can also be used if more subs are needed during a war. Governments of other countries can pay to use a retired U.S. sub for a certain length of time.

Retired subs might also be used for research purposes, or for Navy experiments. They might even be intentionally sunk in the sea and used for target practice! Practice-shooting torpedoes at actual subs helps build skills among submarine crew members.

Still other subs become historic memorials. They are like floating museums. The USS *Nautilus*, the world's first nuclear-powered sub, is one example. It is part of the U.S. Navy Force Museum in Groton, Connecticut. There, visitors can walk through the *Nautilus* and see how crewmen lived and worked at sea.

In a modular system, each part that makes up the system can easily be removed and replaced without taking apart the entire system. This makes improving the technology on board a faster and easier project.

Navy SEALs are ready for ▼ their mission inside an ASDS vehicle attached to the USS *Philadelphia* in 2005.

The Advanced SEAL Delivery System (ASDS) will make the missions of the Navy's special forces, or SEALs, safer and more successful. The ASDS is a small underwater vehicle which is launched from a fast-attack sub. The ASDS carries Navy SEALs and their equipment quickly and silently. It also contains surveillance, or spying, equipment. This allows the SEALs to check out the shore on which they are about to land, before they actually leave the vehicle.

Whatever other new technology comes along in the future, the mission of America's submarines will stay the same. They will search, observe, and protect. And they will use the darkness beneath the waves to carry out their missions in secrecy.

Chapter SIX

Training and Skills

It takes a special kind of sailor to serve on a submarine. Those who serve on subs are some of the most highly-trained and skilled people in the Navy. Everyone on board, no matter what his job is, must know how to operate, maintain, and repair the major systems on board the sub.

They must know how to work the electrical systems, the nuclear reactor, the sonar equipment, the weapons systems, and how to drive the sub. They must also be able to work as cooks and store clerks.

Crewmen on a sub must also be able to live in a small space, often for months at a time. They must be able to get along with a hundred or so other people living and working very closely together.

No sailor in the Navy is ever forced to serve on a sub. Those that are there, want to be there. But not everyone who wants to be on a sub gets to serve on one. Sailors who request submarine duty undergo psychological testing to see if they can handle the cramped living space. These tests also help to find out if sailors can work closely with the others on board the subs while being submerged.

A working submarine and its crew is the result of the efforts of many specially-trained people. The vessel itself is the result of the great skill of submarine designers and technicians. The design of a sub must allow it to move smoothly through deep water. Because of the limited space, the interior design must use every inch of space efficiently.

Those who serve on subs are some of the most highly-trained and skilled people in the Navy.

Great engineering skill is also needed to create the sonar, weapons, day-to-day living, and other systems on board.

In addition to the technical, engineering, and scientific skill that goes into the creation and smooth operation of a submarine, human skill is needed as well. Crewmen must operate, maintain, and repair the equipment. The captain must command the vessel, taking into account the needs of the mission, the needs of the crew, and the capability of the submarine. And the crew must work as a team.

Training

Every crew member on board a sub has undergone months of training. Crew members learn to operate the submarine's systems and equipment in a

▼ A sailor gets some hands-on practice repairing a leak at the Submarine Training Facility in Norfolk, Virginia.

All submarine crewmen must be able to operate and repair all ▲ of the main systems on the sub. These sailors are working on the USS *Georgia* while it is docked at San Diego, California.

classroom, and then they practice on board a sub while still in port. In addition, interactive training manuals on computers give an in-depth look at all a crewman needs to know.

Virtual reality trainers are also used in the teaching of submarine crewmen. Wearing virtual reality goggles, students sit at a model of a submarine control room, weapons stations, and communications station. Trainees practice piloting a sub in and out of port. They practice submerging and bringing a sub back to the surface.

Submarines: Underwater Stealth

The virtual reality system can change the conditions a trainee faces in the scene he is working with. It can alter the weather, ocean conditions, and the presence of other vessels. It can also create crisis situations, such as accidents on board or attacks by opposing subs or ships. This teaches the trainee how to react to different

▼ A simulator is another way a submarine crewman trainee can practice operating a sub. He operates a control panel while the simulator imitates the feel of the sub moving through the water.

FACTFILE

Why No Women?

There are no women assigned to submarine crews. This is because there is so little space on board a sub that there is no way to give men and women their own privacy during a long voyage. Women do come aboard for short assignments and to visit family members when submarines are in port.

situations, which gives him valuable experience before heading out to sea.

Final training comes during test runs at sea. There, combat situations are simulated. Torpedoes without explosives are fired, sonar is monitored to detect the presence of opposing vessels, and stealth surveillance is practiced.

Careers

When they get out of the Navy, many crewmen who served on subs work in technical jobs. They take care of and repair engines on cars, boats, or planes. They also can work in the communications field, operating technical broadcasting equipment. Many submarine sailors and officers use their knowledge of nuclear systems to find jobs working at nuclear power plants. Their training and experience as part of a special group living and working under the sea, operating sophisticated, specialized equipment, helps them do many kinds of jobs.

ballast tanks—Tanks on a submarine which fill with air to keep the sub afloat and fill with water to help it submerge.

berthing area—The place where submarine crewmen sleep.

bunker—A reinforced room made of steel and concrete, sometimes underground, used for protection during a battle.

cruise missile—Weapon that flies through the air to strike a target on land.

decommission—To put out of service.

decompression—Changes in pressure.

hull—The outer skin of a ship or submarine.

intelligence—Information about a country's military plans and weapons.

noise signature—The sound a submarine or ship makes in the water, unique to each vessel.

periscope—A device on a submarine that sticks out of the water and allows the crew to see what is happening on the surface, while the sub is still underwater.

radar—Radio waves sent out to locate objects on the ground or in the air.

sonar—Equipment on a submarine which sends out sound waves to locate objects underwater or to listen to the sounds made by other submarines or ships.

submerge—To go underwater.

surface—To rise up to the top of a body of water.

surveillance—Watching in secret, spying.

torpedo—Weapon carried by submarines, meant to move underwater and strike another sub or a ship.

vertical launch tube—Metal tube aimed to fire a weapon into the air.

Books

DiMecurio, Michael, and Michael Benson. *The Complete Idiot's Guide to Submarines.* Indianapolis: Alpha Books, 2003.

Higgins, Christopher. *Nuclear Submarine Disasters.* New York: Chelsea House, 2001.

Humble, Richard, and Mark Bergin. *A World War II Submarine.* New York: Peter Bedrick Books, 2001.

Hutchinson, Robert. *Jane's Submarines: War Beneath the Waves from 1776 to the Present Day.* New York: HarperCollins, 2002.

Mallard, Neil. *Submarines.* New York: Dorling Kindersley, 2003.

Payan, Gregory, and Alexander Guelke. *Life on a Submarine.* Danbury, Conn.: Children's Press, 2000.

Walker, Sally M. *Secrets of a Civil War Submarine: Solving the Mysteries of the* H. L. Hunley. Minneapolis: Carolrhoda, 2005.

Wingate, Brian. *Submarines: Life in Submarines.* New York: Rosen, 2003.

Internet Addresses

http://science.howstuffworks.com/submarine.htm
The "How Stuff Works" Web site gives details on how a submarine works.

http://www.chinfo.navy.mil/navpalib/cno/n87/n77.html
A Navy Web site with information about submarines from the past and present.

http://www.ussnautilus.org/archive.html
The Web site of the Submarine Force Museum in Groton, Connecticut.

INDEX